A Tribute to
THE YOUNG AT HEART

TOMIE DE PAOLA

By Julie Berg

Published by Abdo & Daughters, 4940 Viking Drive Suite 622, Edina, Minnesota 55435.

Library bound edition distributed by Rockbottom Books, Pentagon Tower, P.O. Box 36036, Minneapolis, Minnesota 55435.

Cover photo -   Globe
Photo credits -   Globe - pgs. 5, 15, 24, 29
                   Bettmann - pgs. 10-11

Edited by Rosemary Wallner

LIBRARY OF CONGRESS CATALOGING-IN-PUBLICATION DATA
Berg, Julie.
    Tomie de Paola / written by Julie Berg.
        p.   cm. -- (Young at Heart)
    Includes bibliographical references and index.
    Summary: Presents the life of the author-illustrator who has won numerous awards and prizes, including the Caldecott Medal, for his children's books.
    ISBN 1-56239-223-9
    1. De Paola, Tomie -- Biography -- Juvenile literature. 2. Authors-illustrators -- United States -- Biography -- Juvenile literature. [1. De Paola, Tomie. 2. Authors, American. 3. Illustrators.] I. Title. II. Series.
    PS3554.E5924Z55   1993
    813.54--dc20   93-12960
    [B]   CIP
                                                 AC

TABLE OF CONTENTS

A BLEND OF
FACT AND FANTASY

The year 1978 was a good one for Tomie de Paola (pronounced de-POW-la). Children across the United States chose four of his books as their favorites. No other creator of children's books in 1978 was given such an honor.

De Paola is one of the most delightful and entertaining children's authors of our time. His books have won many awards. Adults as well as young people enjoy them.

De Paola writes and illustrates his books in his own whimsical sytle. His books blend fact and fantasy and humor to create interesting characters and storylines.

Most importantly, Tomie de Paola cares about children and the books which are produced for them.

Tomie de Paola, one of the most beloved authors
and illustrators of children's books.

"It's a dream of mine that one of my books, any book, any picture, will touch the heart of some individual child and change that child's life for the better, " he said. "I don't even have to know about it. I hope it's not a far-fetched dream. Meanwhile, I'll keep working, doing the best I'm capable of."

BEGINNINGS

Thomas Anthony "Tomie" de Paola was born on September 15, 1934, in Meriden, Connecticut. His father was a barber. In the 1930s, the Great Depression affected Americans. Banks closed and many people were unemployed. De Paola's father was lucky enough to find work.

At a young age, de Paola knew he wanted to be a writer. From the time he started school, he wanted to be on stage, write words, and draw pictures for books. "I must have been a stubborn child," he said, "because I never swayed from that decision."

De Paola attributes this desire to his childhood experiences in his hometown.

"Maybe it was the size of the town," he recalled. "Or maybe it was the fact that my tap dancing lessons were reported in the newspaper. But I remember loving that town because everybody knew me. I was the best artist from about fourth grade on, and the yearbook said so. I had made the decision to be an artist and author of books when I was four."

His mother also had a strong influence over him. She read aloud to the family every night. That, de Paola said, had a much do with his decision to become an artist.

"She would read the old fairy tales and legends," he recalled. "I would come down, not able to sleep, and see my mother curled up in a chair with graham crackers and peanut butter, reading," he said.

Tomie de Paola entered the first grade in 1941. He was an eager student. But school didn't always excite him.

"First grade was great except for 'Dick and Jane,' "
he said. "I hated them." But he loved reading and
got a library card. He began to spend time in the
children's wing of the library. He fell in love with
three things at the library. He loved the books, a
mural of knights and princesses, and a large framed
map of fairyland.

De Paola's first-grade teacher also helped shape his
interest in books. "Mildred Kiniry was my teacher,"
he said. "I adored her. She let me draw and read
and tell her things. I told her I was going to be an
artist when I grew up—and sing and dance on stage.
She suggested I might consider being a lawyer. I
guess my arguing every point with her was quite
impressive!"

As a child, de Paola had an exceptional memory. He
could sing any song after hearing it once. He could
memorize any poem, and tell the plot of any movie.
But math gave him problems. He could not
memorize his math tables.

That same year, the United States entered World War II. Suddenly, de Paola's lifestyle changed. His father worked the night shift at a factory. De Paola and his mother were home alone much of the time.

"All of a sudden," he recalled, "it became the 'War Years.'" The de Paolas rationed gas and food. They practiced what they would do in case of an air raid. They contributed to scrap and paper drives. They went to rallies where people sold war bonds.

"Those were also the years that my tap dancing really took off," he remembered. De Paola performed in many recitals, benefits, and Lion's Club meetings in town. The money raised from these events were donated to the war effort. "I was terribly patriotic," de Paola said.

In addition to his tap dancing, de Paola kept up with his artwork. While in the fourth grade, he entered his first art contest. He won first prize.

De Paola grew up during World War II.
His father worked in a factory that built equipment for
the war, much like the one shown above.

Walt Disney encouraged young de Paola to keep practicing his art.

That same year, he sent a drawing to film producer Walt Disney. He received a letter from Disney's secretary. According to de Paola, the letter said "how pleased Mr. Disney was to receive my drawing. He said to keep practicing and that to be an artist was a wonderful profession. He asked the secretary to send me back my drawing because he knew how important it was for artists to keep their early work."

Once in high school, de Paola became active in stage productions. He performed onstage as well as working behind the scenes. "I performed in Props and Paints productions," he recalled. "I sang in special chorus. I made posters. I was decoration chairman for the Junior Prom and the Senior Reception. I was art editor for the 1952 annual. I was in every variety show."

LEAVING HIS
CHILDHOOD BEHIND

When he graduated in 1952, de Paola realized his childhood years were over. "I cried and cried and I couldn't stop," he said. "I guess somewhere deep, deep down I knew that my Meriden years were coming to an end. Something was finished and I was frightened. I didn't want it to end."

Things weren't all bad, however. De Paola had won a Maloney Scholarship to the Pratt Institute in New York City. There, he would study to become a professional artist.

But things would never be the same for de Paola. He had to leave the security of his hometown. He had to leave many of his friends and family. He knew he had to grow up.

One of the first things de Paola learned at Pratt was that other artists existed.

"I went off to art school thinking that Norman Rockwell and Jon Whitcombe, famous illustrators at the time, were the zenith," de Paola said. "But I learned to keep my mind open and not make any judgments about things until I knew more about them."

It didn't take de Paola more than a couple of months before he suddenly discovered Picasso, George Rowe, and Matisse. "I said to myself, 'Hey wait a minute. This is something very exciting. I don't know anything about it, but it certainly is appealing to me.' "

Going to Pratt also opened de Paola to more experiences that successful artists often need. "Pratt really didn't have dormitories back then," he said. "So I lived in a room in the Brooklyn neighborhood. I was a kid from a small town and I loved New York. Every Saturday morning, I would get on the subway and go into Manhattan."

He started going to art galleries. He would watch the lights come on and be back in Brooklyn by Saturday night, working away at his drawing board.

De Paola went to Pratt Art School in Manhattan.
He was from a small town but soon came to love New York City.

De Paola found Pratt difficult, but challenging. Pratt prescribed a very strict course of studies. "If you concentrated on illustration," he said, "you had to take what they told you to take—drawing, design, and, eventually, painting. I started with figure drawing. I also did animal and perspective drawing. It wasn't four courses a semester. It was nine to five, five days a week."

In 1955, de Paola earned a scholarship to the Skowhegan School of Painting and Illustration in Maine. In the summer between his junior and senior years, he spent ten weeks in Skowhegan.

There, de Paola was fortunate enough to study with Ben Shahn. Shahn had the most impact on de Paola. "He told me that being an artist was more than the kind of things you do," de Paola recalled. "It's the way you live your life, he told me. I've never forgotten that."

JOINING THE MONASTERY

De Paola graduated from Pratt in 1956. Then he spent six months in a Benedictine monastery. The monastery was on top of a hill in a small village in Vermont. Though it was a small place, it had a good library.

De Paola cut his hair and changed his name. He wore the long robes of the monks every day. When the monks chanted, he chanted, too. "It was like being in a movie," he said.

The monastery gave de Paola a way to view life. It also made him realize that culture was also important. "If you can add to the culture of the race of man," he said, "you're doing a really hot number. It certainly gave me time to delve even more into the study of art. I was sort of the resident artist. I think it also gave me a great deal of respect for work."

De Paola returned to the real world, but maintained his ties with the monastery. He designed fabric for their weaving studio. He even helped them start a Christmas card business.

"Then I began doing all kinds of other art work," he continued, " and was soon able to make my living as an artist. In the summer I worked in summer theater. Then I got married, for about a year-and-a-half. A friend said it was my brief period. I was briefly in the monastery and briefly married."

In 1961, de Paola held a one-man art show in Boston. "It was very exciting to have all your things on the wall and all these people coming over. It went very well. I actually sold stuff. I have to admit I made a fairly nice living from my paintings and drawings."

De Paola moved from Boston to New York in 1962 and began to teach. Whenever he had spare time, he visited companies and showed them his portfolio. Many people rejected his artwork. De Paola became discouraged. He wondered if he would ever be an artist.

In 1964, de Paola got his first big break. He met Florence Alexander, an agent. She took his artwork and showed it to the people she knew. Six weeks later, de Paola was illustrating his first book. It was a picture science book by Lisa Miller titled *Sound*.

Alexander continued to represent de Paola. Before long, another company hired him to illustrate a book. "Before I knew it," he said, "I was off and running."

In 1967, de Paola became restless. He didn't like living in New York anymore. He went back to the monastery. But he stayed an even shorter time than before.

He decided to go to San Francisco, California, and attend graduate school. He wanted to earn a masters degree. He kept teaching but knew he could earn more money with a higher degree. De Paola also wanted to live in a culture totally different than the one he was used to.

De Paola found life in San Francisco exciting. "It was a terrific, walkable city," he said. "In twenty minutes I could be on an isolated beach. It didn't have great museums, but somehow I didn't miss them."

But after four years in California, de Paola returned to New Hampshire in 1971. Life was good in California, but his artwork suffered. The good life made it hard for de Paola to concentrate.

"There was no edge to my life, which I missed," de Paola recalled. "It was very easy living in California. You had work to do, but then you looked out the window and said, 'Gosh, it's so beautiful I think I'll just go for a walk.' "

Once back in New Hampshire, de Paola settled in the small town of Wilmot Flat. Life there was more suited to his profession. He liked the Northeast. The winters, the snow, and the cold weather inspired him and gave him more energy to work. Besides, there were very few distractions.

"The other thing is that when you live in the country, you can have space," he added. "I have an enormous barn. It's a dream studio. I could never afford it in New York, no matter how successful I was or am. But I also travel enough so that I don't get cabin fever and I entertain people who visit me for weekends, which is always terrific."

De Paola now works as an associate professor and artist-in-residence at New England College. He also teaches theater design and has developed a children's theater program at Colby-Sawyer College in New Hampshire. In addition to writing and illustrating more children's books, de Paola often visits schools where he talks to children and reads to them.

THE BOOKS OF
TOMIE DE PAOLA

De Paola has illustrated and written over 160 books. "I started as an illustrator and I still think of myself as an artist first. If I stand in front of the easel or sit at my drawing table and do drawings that aren't book oriented, that's one thing. But in order to do books, I've got to have the words, because I've got to illustrate the words.

"The story comes first," he continued. "The hardest part is to try not to see it in pictures until the story is there, especially if I'm writing it myself. That's extremely important because if it doesn't have a good story, no matter how beautiful the pictures are, it's not going to be a good book."

Charlie Needs a Cloak (1973) was de Paola's first informational book which he both wrote and illustrated. In the story, Charlie shears a sheep, then washes, spins, and dyes the wool. Finally, Charlie weaves, cuts, and sews the cloth. The humorous text makes learning fun—a de Paola trademark.

According to de Paola, the idea for *Charlie Needs a Cloak* appeared one day. He had learned to spin wool and weave when he lived in Vermont so the story flowed simply and naturally. "I feel that if I don't actually get involved personally with my characters, whether they be human or animal, and find some personal characteristics of either myself or my friends in them, they are not 'real,' " he said. "And that is of prime importance to me—that fantasy be 'real,' from the child-in-us-all point of view."

De Paola used his memories of his grandmother and great-grandmother in another book, *Nana Upstairs & Nana Downstairs* (1973). The story concerns de Paola's relationships with his grandmother and great-grandmother and his reactions to their eventual deaths. *Nana Upstairs & Nana Downstairs* is a very important book to me because it's totally autobiographical," he said. Not surprisingly, it is also one of his favorite books.

De Paola modeled many of the characters
in his books after people in his life.

De Paola's Italian grandmother was the model for the heroine in *Watch Out for the Chicken Feet in Your Soup* (1974). "Like Joey's grandmother in the story," he said, "she pinched my cheeks, talked 'funny,' and made Easter bread dolls that were a highlight in my young life.

"There's a lot of me in the character of Joey," he added. "And Joey's friend Eugene is a combination of all my friends through the years who were entranced by my grandmother—her house, accent, and cooking, not to mention the chicken feet."

"She always put chicken feet in my soup," he added. "And I was fascinated. It certainly was something to brag about. You know: 'My Daddy does this.' 'Well, my Daddy does that.' And finally, I could mow down my opponents with 'My Grandma puts chicken feet in the soup!' Da dah! Stardom! I also remember the wonderful moment when my aunts fought over who was going to get the foot floating in the soup.

"My grandmother absolutely believed that everyone was hungry and that everyone must put away tons of food to keep their strength up," he added. "More than once I was paralyzed by a plate of spaghetti that rivaled the print of Mt. Vesuvius on the wall in height."

In 1975, de Paola published *The Cloud Book.* It shows the ten most common types of clouds. It also includes Italian folklore about clouds.

De Paola used his Italian background in another book, *Strega Nona* (1975). *Strega Nona* is a traditional story set in Italy. It is about a magic cooking pot that produces food for the person who knows the correct chant. And it keeps on producing food until it is given a special signal to stop.

Strega Nona (Grandmother Witch) owns the pot. Her houseboy, Big Anthony, knows the chant to start the cooking. But he cannot stop the pot. He turns the little Italian town into a disaster area that is engulfed by pasta. De Paola won a Caldecott Medal for this book. The Caldecott is the highest honor a children's book can receive.

The Popcorn Book emerged in 1978. It remains one of his most popular works. The story begins with two young people getting ready to pop some corn. They begin to wonder where popcorn comes from and how it pops. De Paola mixes fact with Indian legends throughout the book. He writes about little demons in the kernels who get so mad when they get hot that they blow up.

De Paola produces four books a year. Some of his more noteworthy books are *Giorgio's Village* for which he received the Golden Kite award in 1982, and *The Friendly Beasts* (1981) which received the *Boston Globe-Horn Book* honor for its illustrations. Other titles have been named best and notable books by professional organizations. In addition, de Paola has received several prizes for his art and has held many national and international exhibitions.

A MATTER OF COLOR AND STYLE

De Paola puts a lot of color and his own style into his books. "My color is quite distinctive," he said. "I think my style of illustrations has been refined over the years. Style has to do with the kinds of things you are drawn to personally, and I'm drawn to Romanesque and folk art. I think that my style is very close to those—very simple and direct. I simplify."

De Paola has a favorite way to draw his illustrations. "I do my books in watercolor-type mediums," he said. "I used to love painting oils, but I'm allergic to the smell of turpentine. So now when I paint, I use acrylic. My favorite medium is that combinations of tempera-watercolor-acrylic."

"Illustrating and writing has to do with dreams," he added. "A dream that I expressed as a child, that when I grew up I would write and draw pictures for books. A dream that people I've never met would get to know me a little better.

De Paola has enthusiasm, a sense of humor, a
vivid imagination and a genuine love of children.

"A dream that the invisible world could be made visible, and even a dream that I could somehow touch others' lives."

De Paola has enthusiasm, a sense of humor, a vivid imagination—and a genuine love of children. These are the qualities he brings into all of his books. With dazzling illustrations and descriptive words, he makes readers laugh while they learn. And he shows us the world through the eyes of a child, that is, and who always will remain, Tomie de Paola.

GLOSSARY

Benedictine- a monk or nun belonging to the order founded by St. Benedict.

Folklore- traditional beliefs, legends, and tales.

Fundamentalist- a person who believes in the Bible as a factual historical record.

Illustrator- a person who provides drawings for a book.

Meditate- to reflect upon; ponder.

Medium- a specific type of artistic technique.

Monastery- a community of monks.

Romanesque- A style of European art and architecture from the ninth to the twelfth century.

INDEX